War, Not Terrorism

PAT SKINNER

ISBN 978-1-64458-987-8 (paperback)
ISBN 978-1-64458-988-5 (digital)

Christian Faith Publishing, Inc.
832 Park Avenue
Meadville, PA 16335
www.christianfaithpublishing.com

Printed in the United States of America

Contents

Preface

I have put this book together to help inform those interested as to what is going on around the world today in the spiritual sense. I base this view upon facts that are seen, as well as through study. I also bring in biblical scripture and what I believe God has shown me concerning this.

First, I have titled this *War Not Terrorism*. Now what is war? Let us look at the definition.

War: (1a) A state or period of usually open and declared hostile conflict between states or nations. (1b) The art or science of warfare. (2a) A state of hostility, conflict, or antagonism. (2b) A struggle between opposing forces or for a particular end.

In light of the definition, and as you read through the following pages, you'll be able to see how war is being waged against the United States. This war is against our belief system, and the constitution which this country is founded upon. We have seen in the news and on TV how many of the Islamic countries have been chanting, "Down with Israel as well as the United States. Burning our flag and killing and torturing people from countries who disagree with their beliefs."

They are executing Christians and torturing them just for their belief in Jesus Christ. They have punished their own people who even help a Christian. They blow themselves up in the name of their god, which is by the way a religious belief. This is actually spiritual warfare being carried out through people who have a god who hates, is unmerciful, and intolerant. It is satanic and evil.

September 21, 2016. The *Saint Cloud Times* mentions an interfaith dialogue with Somali families. (When I mention this, I am not looking at the people in general. I am looking at their culture and religious beliefs. Let's ask ourselves: do they honor your rights? And respect the laws of the land? Particularly the United States.) This article was to better understand Somali families and to welcome them. This was a meeting of Muslim-Christian dialogue. This gathering was at St. Joseph's rectory in St. Joseph Minnesota. (Catholic church) The goal was to understand more who these people are, what a Muslim ascribes to, and what he believes. They said in the article that it is nothing any Christian should have a problem with, nor they with us. Dianne De Vargas said, "We have some differences of opinions and that hopefully will come out, as far as who our god is." She went further to say, "He is one god and we all believe in one god." This is the unifying thing among us. That's pretty much the goal. They had a table discussion as well as a break so the Muslims could pray and have refreshments.

Other churches in St. Joseph include resurrection Lutheran, and the Gateway church have joined in uniting.

This is an assimilating process, and the church members in these churches claim to have the same god as Islam. The Christian church has Jesus, and the Muslims have Muhammad their prophet, not the Son of God!

They will be explained in the following chapters. Do not think and believe as Americans do. Airports have made special prayer rooms for them to pray. Some apartment buildings, other tenants aren't allowed to put up any Christmas wreaths or merry Christmas signs because the Muslims are offended. Can you see this? Offended at our religious beliefs. They are offended when someone wants to honor the birth of Jesus. And then they are welcomed with open arms. Their complaint is a religious one. It interferes with their belief and goes against the teachings of the Imams and their prophet, Muhammad. St. Cloud State University had a united march. This was after a Muslim attacked people with a knife at the Crossroads mall in St Cloud. He did this in the name of his god Al-ah—a religious belief again. Kill the infidel with a knife. There were more than three hundred people at the march as well as speakers and discussion groups.

The United States passed a law in the fifties not to allow any Muslims into the country because of their treatment toward woman. Now they are cheerfully welcomed and given special treatment and rights that regular Americans don't have. This is because leaders are bowing to their religious beliefs. This is not just the Somalians, it is also the Syrians and other Muslim countries. They have a plan through their hierarchy to assimilate and move into government. This is the political side of Islam; they have a goal.

January 1, 2017. There was a Muslim affairs banquet in California honoring the Muslim women that were working with Obama and the mayor of New York.

The woman working with Obama was Rumada Ahmed. She received an award for her work with Muslims in the White House. She was the national security strategic communications advisor.

She spoke also about working with the Cubans and Moracins.

Sarah Sied the advisor for the New York mayor works with Catholic charities to create dialog. She is also the senior community affairs advisor. She says, "They want to align Islamic law with civil law." She is the advisor on rights. There were five others also honored. They were supported by Rep. Ted Lieu of California. He said he would be their voice in congress and was fighting for them.

Note: See how they are using women to infiltrate. In their religion, women are subject to the control of men. Even if you live around them, you see very few men even working in the yard etc. Women are lowered, and they use them to do most of the work.

Jan 3, 2017. Minnesota swore in another Somalian lawmaker Liham Omar as representative. These people have a plan. In this country, they can't get away with what they do in others because of our laws. Countries where Islam rules, they kill you, and you go right to trial. In this country, they are moving to change the laws and constitution. They moved in politically, and this is happening right before the eyes of the American people. Others are already working with Obama in the White House, or through it with homeland security, as well as educational areas in this country. I am not saying they are all Somalians; they are Ishmaelites dedicated to the goals of Islam and Sharia law, a religious constitution for world domination in the name of Allah.

Many of our leaders and people of this country that are working with them are not even aware of their motive and the spirit behind the beliefs of Islam. Many of the people of Germany didn't see what Hitler was doing 'till it was too late. I hope this inspires you to check out all the areas of this religious move by the enemy through Islamic doctrine.

Introduction to Terrorism

First, acknowledging something and that is what we are actually dealing with in relation to what is going on in the world and the church. We will be looking at what is going on and has been going on, and has been moving into the United States. We must first see a war is being waged against the principles, values, and the constitution of the United States.

If this being the case, then we are faced with a combat situation. First question: What are the goals of the enemy? What does the enemy think is correct? What are the weapons the enemy uses to try and defeat you and this nation? These are but a few questions we must ask ourselves. I will attempt to answer and explain some of these questions in the next few chapters. Chapter one, we will look at terrorism first. The reason for this is we have heard this used so much in relation to what is going on in the world. It has generated much anxiety in many people. We will examine this and the purpose of it. We are dealing with the spiritual here.

What Is Terrorism?

We are looking at Islam here in relation to the spirit behind that religious or constitutional belief.

Terrorism is actually a tool used in their form of warfare. There are actually two sides to Islam. One is political manipulation, and the other is the warrior side. The warriors or fighters use terror as a means of creating fear. This causes many to just fall in and follow. The political side falls into the category of influencing political leaders, and politicians to take their side and make and enforce laws upon the people if they won't acknowledge them. In the United States, now, many leaders in this country who are not thinking spiritually bow to these demands and used (could say misuse) or misinterpret the constitution and rights and use them against the citizens of this country. This is someone else gaining control of government. The constitution was drawn up for the United States and pertains to this republic, and country, the people who are citizens here—not the entire world. (If others want these same rights, give them a copy of the constitution for their own country.) We hear often the term radical Islam. Let' look at the term radical.

Radical: first, it relates to the origin, also extreme, to include or relating to, or constituting a political group associated with views, practices and policies of extreme change.

Islam means submission. Let's look at policies first. The White House under Obama has placed Muslims in positions to influence decisions concerning the welfare of the citizens and welfare of the United States as well as the world. If you notice the rights in regards to speech concerning the beliefs of Islam, they call it hate speech. Yes, you are punished, or it's called a crime. They have moved into government. and now laws are in place to promote the welfare and the ongoing of Islam in the United States. When there is a tragic situation concerning, let's say the beheading of Christians or Non-Muslims, they are called radical. That is a form of terror. When we see it done through the manipulating of laws, we are seeing the political side where the leaders and people voluntarily submit. This is classified as peaceful. But at the same time, it is submission to Al-ah and Islam. I hope you can see this. There are now Muslims involved with homeland security, the security advisory council, faith-based neighborhood partnerships (we see this with that St. Joseph church) and many more areas of this government. (To get more info on this, you can check out the book by Shira Sorko-Ram titled *The Secret Radical Plot to Conquer America*) So now we have seen a small portion of the political side.

The leaders who approve the ideas of Islam are blind to the spiritual side of what they are agreeing with or to. The United States was not built on the beliefs of Islam, not Roman Catholic or communistic ideas. It has been founded upon the Bible and a scriptural government where people could worship God and Jesus Christ. A foundation of love for God and his ways. Islam is based upon Al-ah, Muhammad, and the foundation of old testament law, and ones they have made up. President Obama has often spoken of his love for the prayers of Islam and has shown favor in the direction of Islam and the Koran. He has shown more concern for the things and issues outside of the United States and America. The US has helped more countries and nations than any other; we have sent more missionaries also. We now have seen a different value system coming in and catering to those who hold a different belief than what this nation was founded upon. One big thing is that the Muslims seem to always be complaining about being treated unfairly. We see the "elected" government officials forcing the citizens of their own country to bow to the desires of people who have different gods, values, and ungodly ideas and practices. This is done through the making of laws, and the Muslims are interacting with the lawmakers to passively force the people to submit and deny their own faith or keep it to yourself. Tax dollars go to bring these people over here and also used to change and enact laws contrary to the constitution of the United States while supporting the ungodly.

Much of what Islam is doing has also been done by the holy Roman Catholic church. That is why the first settlers came to America, to escape papal authority. This is after the pope declared himself the ruler of the conscience of all men and infallible (meaning he can't make a mistake). The people wanted to worship God and Jesus Christ according to the dictate of their own heart. Many coming to this country today aren't coming to worship Jesus or God; they are bringing their religion here and fighting to change this country to bow down to their god Allah. Thus causing many Americans to lose their lives and depleting the US of much of its resources.

Next, politics defined is the art or science of government. Guiding or influencing government policy, or of winning and holding control over a government.

Terrorism is then one of the weapons used against this country. The lawmakers in turn approve funds to countries that produce, harbor, and support ideologies contrary to Christianity and the constitution of the US. This has progressively gotten worse.

 It is a war against decency. The courts have ordered the Ten Commandments out of schools, which the laws in this country are based on.

The leaders who support this kind of stuff have taken control of government. They argue and fight to change and misinterpret the constitution to fit their global agenda. They make the US constitution apply to anyone from anywhere. The devil is behind this move. It is spoken of in the sense of the US, but the leaders are seeing this as global. This globalization in reality is a move for worldwide communist control with a handful of men in charge. George Bush senior said, "You will have a one world government whether you like it or not." President Obama spoke of a one world collective religion. This is showing us what those in control are aiming at. A one world government, as well as a one world religion, with a one world banking system to control the finances. This is about the self-proclaimed elite controlling everything and keeping the people separate from themselves.

In Revelation 17:3–4, the woman (not the bride of Christ) was full of names of blasphemy. In verse four, the golden cup in her hand (communion chalice) full of abominations. We see at this point how the religions of the world and its system is working with the government to achieve world peace. The devil always appears to have something that will benefit mankind. Then it is a political system with rules while religion on the other hand ease the people's minds or comforts and counsels them. You see them trying to unite Islam with Christianity. This is all part of a satanic plan to destroy the church. Many churches have already submitted to some of these ideas.

Introduction to Communism

⊸⊶⊷∞⊶⊷

I n chapter two, we will be examining communism.
Many folks today have never read the *Communist Manifesto*. What is a manifesto? It is a public declaration of policy, purpose, or views. Manifestation is an expression. "The act, process, or an instance of manifesting. Also a public demonstration of power and purpose." President Obama also used the term appointing czars. A czar was a ruler of Russia until the 1917 revolution. It also means, "One having great power or authority." I find it interesting how it was used in a country that has a scriptural constitution, a nation under God.

We will find out the plan to destroy the family and its values.

Going global and the elimination of countries and borders.

Unions and policies to control companies and businesses beyond simple safety regulations.

Graduated income taxes
See for yourself
The ideas behind communism
Its goals and plans
Decide for yourself
If you see it rearing its head
In the United States
And see who may be promoting it.

KARL MARX
FREDERICK ENGELS

MANIFESTO
OF THE
COMMUNIST PARTY

Written between December 1847
and January 1848

Original in German

First published as a pamphlet
in London in Febrùary 1848

Communism

There are as you know many people never take time to read, study, or research what is going on around them or in the world. The average person likes to assume all people are good and have good intentions. That man is basically good. This is not correct according to scripture found in the Bible, Genesis 6:5, "God saw that every imagination of the thoughts of his heart was only evil continually." When we are looking at this, we are looking at a spiritual condition.

We are looking at self-centeredness. We are seeing man saying inside I don't need God. It doesn't necessarily mean people did bad things to everyone. Again, we are looking at a spiritual condition. I will use for an example homosexuality. If any of them are approached with God does not approve of that, something within them causes them to rise up and say you hate them, or God loves me, or I can do what I want.

When we look at Leviticus 18:22; lying with mankind as with a woman is an abomination. The reason for this is God created and made all things to reproduce after their kind. This activity is against nature itself which reproduces. This stems from a spirit and is a spiritual problem.

God gave this information of what he approves of because he loves us. He was dealing with people in the natural realm who needed to be given this information. It wasn't in them spiritually. The response from people who approve of this activity is something that comes from their own desires. I am not condemning anyone here; I hope you understand this.

Because of the lack of study and seeking truth, it opens the door for the enemy to creep into governments, churches, and influence individuals. Many who never study or check things out can tell you a lot about sports, movies, video games, and new songs but nothing about scripture and what has crept into the church. There is a spiritual battle going on. In 2001, Jesus was even taken out of the big book of Alcoholics Anonymous, and it was and is God and Jesus Christ who gives you the victory over that bondage.

Communism hates God, hates the family, and family values. This is all covered over with what they call your rights and is presented as with best interest for society and the world.

The *Communist Manifesto* was put together by Karl Marx and Frederick Engels. In February 1848, a communist pamphlet was first published in London. This was written between December 1847 and January 1848. In this manifesto (which we now know as a public declaration of policy and view), it states, "It is their desire to abolish countries and nationalities." (Globalism)

You can see this touch of communism even with the pope. "Build bridges to your country." I don't protect it. The man that has been elected president of the richest religious organization on earth says use your finances that you work for to support anyone who chooses to enter your country. He is saying your money, your land, your nation is for anyone who wants to come, and you should take care of them and show them favor regardless. At this point also, I would like to mention, "It is the Roman Catholic church" that is allowed to operate in all the communist countries. They help make the government rich, as well as control the people religiously. Many of the policy makers have this same view. The pope has his own country, and he won't allow just anybody to just move in and live.

The manifesto also states that working men have no country. We cannot take from them what they have not got. It goes further to say, "The proletariat [wage earners] first must acquire political supremacy." They must be the leading class of a nation.

This is not the bourgeois (land and business owners)—this begins with unions. Getting the workers to control who owns the business and drive costs up and in the process, create more federal regulations. This causes the wage earner to destroy their own workplace themselves and rights, leading eventually to poverty.

Another part states, "The first step is in the revolution." (You see this with the instigators starting protests. Now you see this against everything from race to job discrimination.) A revolution by the working class is to raise the proletariat to the position of ruling class to win the battle of democracy. (Notice how it is used to influence the people to think it is in their best interest. While the underlying motive is to destroy the nation using people to do it themselves. This in the process gives more power to government and makes it bigger.)

It goes further to say, "These measures would be different in different countries. In advanced countries: abolition of property in land and application of all rents of land to public purposes." [Notice: Monies earned from rent and made off the land taken and used by the government to distribute however the communist lawmakers feel it should be distributed.)

Remember Obama speaking about redistribution of wealth? Why all the US funds going to nations that hate us? Well what about the farmers?

2. A heavy progressive or graduated income tax. (Could this be how or what they use to take more money?) This funds a larger government and more projects toward globalism and a world government system.

3. Abolition of full rights of inheritance. (Meaning nothing of value can be left to you. You are heavily taxed, or it becomes part of the state. We notice the second proposal a graduated income tax. This refers to intervals, a progression, not all at once.) It is too easy to get caught. They also call themselves the progressives and a progressive movement.

4. Confiscation of property of all immigrants and rebels. (The key word here is rebels. A rebel is someone who disagrees with their ideas. Someone the lawmakers determine to be a rebel. They write

the laws and define them.) They also use the armies and police to enforce what they decree. You see this already in operation in many places. Even in DWI cases, they will take your vehicle. I am not promoting drinking and driving; this is an illustration.

They have to start somewhere (with the rebels right).

Even if you are found not guilty, try to get it back.

5. Centralization of credit in the hands of the state by means of a national bank with state capital and exclusive monopoly. (Note here a monopoly is exclusive ownership or control through legal privilege, command of supply or concerted action. [concerted action refers to an agreement upon plan.] Commodity controlled by one party, a person, or group having a monopoly. Notice also legal privilege. These people with control of the finances get legal privilege. They endorse candidates and lobbyists. Through these means, the lawmakers and politicians, they endorse work for them—not in the best interest of the nation.

Again note here: concerted action relates to a plan or arrangement; something that is mutually contrived or agreed upon. Who are those then that endorse candidates? Those with the money. This is to have things go their direction. One person cannot be the ultimate dictator; this has never actually really worked. Now what is hidden? A group that has influenced lawmakers and controls businesses through regulations. If you think about it, what does war really produce? It generates income for the ones who get the contracts for bullets, bombs, weapons, uniforms, vehicles, aircraft, and things like that at the cost of lives while they achieve financial gain and wealth.

They get a comfortable life and make more money to keep their control and pay their instigators. These people are not just politicians. They are the ones who influence politicians and instigate wars. They have no allegiance to any particular country or nation. This is why this move is for global control. The devil is behind this move. That is why they are opposed to the family, nation, and God. It is war against love and godly values. It states in the Bible 1 Timothy 6:10, "The love of money is the root of *all* evil." This is not saying money is evil. Money can be used for good. (Before moving on, I suggest you research whose lawyers drew up the tax laws for the US Remember, a graduated in come tax. This is progressive. What some of the candidates call themselves. They are hiding what they are doing.)

6. Centralization of the means of communication and transport in the hands of the state. What does this mean? The means of communication relates to how it is done. Referring to news broadcasts, newspapers, the media! Here you can see how they are biased toward one party or the other.

Also one idea or another, they always use someone who is classified as a professional. This is about controlling what the public hears. In a sense, it is actually a form of mind control. Attempting to put the nations thoughts upon their ideas and solutions to world problems they have created. Again, their ideas appear to have your best interest in mind. This is a form of deception to hide their agenda in relation to global control. This is a big worldwide move; it is almost hard to believe, but it is right in front of the faces of the American people what is going on.

7. Extension of factories and instruments of production owned by the state; the bringing into cultivation of waste lands and the improvement of the soil generally in accordance with a common plan. This plan falls into their agreement in relation to control. Even on your own property, the state controls what you can and can't do. See this III. What is wasteland?? Well, whatever the state calls wasteland.

8. Equal liability of all to labor and establishment of industrial armies, especially for agriculture.

Notice the control of farmlands and the crops they produce. These large companies owned by these people, or corporations buy their own products from their own companies at a higher rate and profit. When the normal farmer goes to sell his, they can regulate what he makes. They can say the demand is low, and the price is lowered forcing them to pay more to grow their crops or manufacture their product. There may be a number of people holding stock, but you can rest assured they hold the controlling number of shares. This is about controlling and regulating everything. Also if a farmer is forced to put up his land and farm for collateral on a loan, the controlled bank owns his farm 'till the debt is paid. So they try keep them in debt.

9. Combination of agriculture with manufacturing industries; gradual abolition of the distinction between town and country, by more equable distribution of the population over the country. (Distribution over the country was not in the original but was added later.) How could this be done? Subtly at first, by starting new enterprises in different parts of the country. Just an example: North Dakota with the oil. People flock to where they can make money. Then when they get there cut on the jobs after a set time period and then make it look like something else is the reason, they will usually say the economy which refers again to money. It is a manipulation.

Rise and fall of prices through control in relation to production cost. Combining agriculture with manufacturing, you can see if you look at many products including food come from China or other countries.

The US then becomes a consumer nation and not the manufacturer or producer of the goods. Where do the finances come from to keep buying when many are forced from the labor field? Other countries then get rich off what the US consumes.

10. Free education for all children in public schools. Abolition of children's factory labor in its present form. Combination of education with industrial production, etc. When in the course of development, class distinctions have disappeared, and all production has been concentrated in the hands of a vast association of the whole nation. The public power will lose its political character. Political power, properly so-called, is merely the organized power of one class for oppressing another. If the proletariat during its contest with the bourgeois is compelled by the force of circumstances to organize itself as a class, if by means of revolution, it makes itself the ruling class, and as such, sweeps away by force the old conditions of production, then it will along with these conditions have swept away the conditions for the existence of class antagonisms and of classes generally and will thereby have abolished its own supremacy as a class. In place of the old bourgeois society, with its class antagonisms, we shall have an association in which the free development of each is the condition for the free development of all. You can see this playing out with candidates who are running for office. Free education is the only part they use.

Why? The media is controlled. This appeals to the people because it appears to have their best interest in mind again along with their children while supposedly easing the burden of expense on the family.

They have had school before, and it's been paid for by tax dollars. Who are all these children? When you are thinking globally, it is anyone from any country at the taxpayers' expense, even to people who have no regard for America or its Bible-Based constitution. They used to teach history, reading, writing, arithmetic, and values. They had the ten commandments in schools. They were taken down because a judge said the children might read them and believe them. This is what our laws are based on!

At this point, I will go back to 1836, eleven years before the Communist Manifesto was written. There were a handful of American intellectuals.

They each had mutual interests and met at Harvard's bicentennial celebration. There they discussed their new philosophical trends. These folks formed what is historically known as the transcendentalist movement. Some of these transcendentalists were Ralph Waldo Emerson, Henry Thoreau, Bronson Alcott, and Margaret Fuller. They felt something was missing which was an invisible dimension of reality. I don't feel their intentions were evil. At this time in history, you had the church but in a more religious and superstitious state. The revival which took place on Azusa Street hadn't happened yet. This is where many began speaking in tongues, and the Spirit had fallen on these believers as they were praying. This upset mainstream religion, and many said it was of the devil, just as some still think that today.

The transcendentalists called this dimension the over-soul. They began to look to understand this and sought it out through a number of sources. Experience, intuition, the Quaker ideas of inner light, the Bhagavad Gita, historian Thomas Carlyle, Samuel Coleridge the poet, along with several English metaphysical writers of the seventeenth century. The transcendentalists affected literature, education, politics, and economics for many generations.

They influenced Nathaniel Hawthorne, Emily Dickinson, Herman Melville, Walt Whitman, along with the founders of the British Labor party, Gandhi, and Martin Luther King. To transcend is to move above. This movement was to find your real self. And the true human nature. (We are going to look for a moment at the spiritual side. This would be pure humanism, or man without God. Organized religion sets people on this course of searching and in the process finds what man's nature is without God, destructive and judgmental.)

Now back to the schools or educational system. The changers of society are aiming at a new world and society. The visionaries have said, "If you change the education of the younger generation is the only way you can have a new society." Yet the new society itself is the necessary force for the change in education. They state, "Schools are bureaucracies whose practitioners do not compete for business, do not need to get re-elected, or to attract patients, customers, or clients." The consumer cannot simply boycott this institution. It is illegal in many states to remove your children from these institutions. (Can you see this control to influence the children with things like common core?)

And remove and change history among other ungodly things. Well, they finally removed the pledge of allegiance. In the survey of these conspirators, it was found more were involved in education than any other category of work. They were teachers, administrators, policy makers, and educational psychologists.

One expressed it as a "peaceful struggle" within the system. Marrio Fantini, former Ford consultant on education said bluntly, "The psychology of becoming has to be smuggled into the schools." Schools are an effect of the way we think, and we can change the way we think. (More information on this can be found in a book by Marilyn Ferguson, titled *The Aquarian Conspiracy*, 1980) Marrio Fantini is saying then that the peoples thinking must be changed to agree with their ideas in relation to educating their children. Note here, Revelation 20:7–8, "Satan shall go out and deceive the nations." Also 2 Timothy 3:13, "Evil men and seducers shall wax worse and worse, deceiving and being deceived." Verse twelve before this states,

"Those who live Godly In Christ Jesus shall suffer persecution." Who is doing this persecuting?

Those who believe these ungodly ideas, they attack decency, Christ, and good values, as well as the truth. What has crept into the schools? Alternative lifestyles, sex education, (They even approve of little boys thinking they are girls. This is demonic!) They have introduced counselors for any little thing and taken away from the parents the right to speak to their own children. Along with this, many parents don't even believe in God, or acknowledge God in their homes. Many children in turn don't even get a godly example. (Can we see the ideas of communism at work here?) This has promoted violence, homosexuality, and other issues facing children today. The people behind this don't care, and the politicians have sold the citizens of America out to achieve a larger plan of global control. To quote again from their agenda: "The communists have not invented the intervention of society in education." They do but seek to alter the character of that intervention, and to rescue education from the ruling class. In years past, the parents would have rose up against what is now going on in the schools. We can now see how the indoctrination over time has eroded the values and moral codes that once were. Disrespect instead of respect toward teachers and parents. If they do what the student doesn't like, they turn the parent or teacher over to a counselor or the courts. See 2 Timothy 3:1–4 and in verse two—unthankful and disobedient to parents.

Recall again what the judge did. He had the Ten Commandments removed because children might read them and believe them. That is an ungodly judge! The ruling class used to be Christian or have Christian values. It is easy to see how the enemy has been using his people to manipulate society to remove God from this country. They, the communists, say further, "Concerning the bourgeois claptrap about the family and education, about the hallowed co-relation of parent and child is 'disgusting'" (The bourgeois class are the wage earners, or anyone owning property).

They state, "Communism abolishes eternal truth, it abolishes all religion and all morality, instead of constituting them on a new basis; it therefore acts in contradiction to all past historical experience."

Let's look here for a bit at how does the national council of churches fit into the picture through agreeing with the communist pagan system.

Article 2 of the church council defines, "Anything done in the name of, or on the behalf of any religious body, sect, teaching, or personal revelation, or that which creates mistrust, fears, alarm, panic, hatred of or toward, or for any other religious and or political body, belief or conviction when such shall result from Appeals to the superstitious, the supernatural or when unsupported by the accepted religious or political usage as established by law." Now it is easy to see how the law is also used to regulate the message in the churches. This is a ploy of the devil to stop the power of God and the truth. The devil uses his messengers for this. Note: 2 Corinthians 11:13–14, "He transforms his messengers into the preachers of righteousness." See how communistic ideas here abolish eternal truths. This has crept into the churches of mainstream religion.

We have all heard of the health care act. I wonder if many have connected this also with mental health? (NIMH, the national institute on mental health) They have established the standards for a healthy mental attitude on moral conduct and religion. They also have set the standard for health education and welfare. The standard they have set down parallels the national council of churches creed with respect to salvation, divinity, literalism in Bible interpretation, chastity before marriage, abstinence from homosexuality, and heterosexual relationships. These will be spelled out as signs of actual or potential mental illness. Notice what they are saying! How many agree with them?

They are saying if you think it is wrong to be a homosexual, and you have faith in God and Jesus Christ, you are mentally ill or potentially mentally ill.

Now to the woman's movement (I hope this isn't taken wrong. Look at what it is about.) They are looking for an open community of women. Here you see them taking women out of the home, telling them they are worthless. They should be free to do whatever they want to do; they are women. They are just as good as men etc. They are indirectly told that they are worthless in the home and with a family. This is a ploy to destroy the family unit and cause divisions. It breaks down the security of the children and the bonding aspect of the family that the mother brings. This puts children into state-regulated daycare. Career has become more important now. Divorce rates escalate, and women begin to hate their children. Many cases now of the mothers actually killing their children. Abortions rise. A fact is that a nation with strong family values and morals is hard to destroy. It appears it has gone from a family that is married to just living together and calling it a family. Taking God and godly values out of schools and family destroys the hope and gratitude in a nation. It then turns to survival and self-centeredness.

The children have a desire to belong to something, possibly a gang. Suicides among children have gone up, right along with them shooting one another on a frequent basis in many areas. When the regulators control the media with these ungodly ideas of what is good or bad, you can see the desensitizing of people to life itself. They portray more graphic vengeance and violence, especially in video games. This is all a plan to destroy the US, or should I say this country and the gospel and people with godly values and a desire to help others. The United States has given aid to more countries and nations and has sent more missionaries out than any other country. The leaders have joined the United Nations and have given them a say concerning what should be done with support money from the citizens of the US. These leaders have made agreements with devils! Especially when they fight the gospel of Jesus Christ, and the power of God to raise a nation up and protect the people if they will turn to him. These other nations are cursed; because at one time, they had the message of the gospel and have turned their back on God. Psalm 9:17, "The wicked shall be turned into hell, and all nations that forget God." You can also check out Isaiah 60:12 and Jeremiah 7:27–28.

The US has been blessed and is blessed because the Christians are allowed to worship God through Jesus Christ. This is a nation based upon God's principles. Now we are seeing through these ungodly communistic ideas the trouble created when leaders and judges forget God and his principles in governing a nation. They are approving things that God says destroy nations. The sad thing is that people just sit back in church and put trust in their elected officials and haven't paid attention to what has crept in. They say, "It can't happen here! I The Lord has told us to watch and pray." The Lord said in Matthew 13:25, "While men slept the enemy came in and sowed tares among the wheat." They closed their eyes is what it means. Well, look at what is happening here. Who is paying the price? The people who have been doing nothing, just leaving everything up to their pastor or preacher. They say it is too complicated. I'll just see what happens. It will work itself out. Most of these people persecute and label those who believe in the Lord and try to do something as radically religious people. They probably said that in Rome also. Another organization that has a part in what is going on in America is the Vatican, along with the entire organized religious system governed by men with traditions and religious doctrine.

We are dealing with a spiritual problem which will be covered in another chapter. Of course, what I have presented here is just a small part in relation to the big picture. I feel this is enough to stimulate your thinking to take a look at yourself and make a decision. What do I want to do? What is my part concerning the issues now in America? This is more than going to church; it revolves around faith.

God moves when we move with God. Things are going to go God's way. Some say we will just let it go then. Well, Revelation 3:15–16 says, "I wish you were hot or cold, because if you are lukewarm I will spue you out." What are we doing to do our part? Are we getting faith taught to us by our pastor? Does the pastor even know the Bible or use one? By this, I don't mean quoting a couple verses once in a while. Does he believe Isaiah 53:5 or 1 Peter 2:24? Are you a Son of God or a church member? Does your church say you are a child of God when you receive Christ or when you get baptized? If they teach you become a child of God when you are baptized as a baby, they don't know the Bible. It is a doctrine of man. The Bible states, "By grace are you saved through faith" (Ephesians).

Introduction to
Islam

ᖙᖙᖙᖙ

In this chapter, we will discover when Islam was born. How it came about and Muhammad becoming their prophet. What the Muslim pantheon represents. Where Ishmael is in the Bible, and why they pray facing Mecca instead of Jerusalem.

Islam

Before going into the life and some history concerning Muhammad, we should see where the Ishmaelites descended from.

Here we must look at Genesis chapter sixteen. This is where we find out Sarai couldn't have children, so she gave Hagar to Abram to produce a child through. Abram and Hagar then had a child, and he was named Ishmael. Hagar was an Egyptian, Sarai's maid. We can see here that they are actually the children or descendants from Abram. (In reference to this note, Abram is used. His name was later changed to Abraham and Sarai to Sarah.) Abraham was a hundred years of age at this time, and in Genesis 17:19, God said, "I will establish my covenant with his seed after him."

We are seeing here it is not Ishmael. Now in Genesis 17:20, we find where Ishmael had twelve sons also (as Jacob did) and God would make him a great nation also and multiply him. We are looking here at a plan and direction God was taking through the old testament. Now we can see where the Israelites have come from.

Muhammad (ibn Abdallah) note here at the end of Muhammad's name al-l-ah. This was a tradition. Tacking on the end of the name to connect it or you with their high god. You notice with Abram naming Ishmael the el on the end of the name. The word god is translated from Elohim or El. Muhammad changed it to all-ah to connect himself to his god. They come up then with one supreme god, and his name is Allah. Muhammad was from the Meccan tribe of Quraysh.

His clan was the Hashim, which wasn't as successful as some of the other clans. The Arabs adopted many of the pagan deities, and gods and were (still are) warring among themselves for their share in the wealth they had accumulated. In about CE 610, Muhammad had his experience with his visitation. Muhammad adapted his religion for the purpose of bringing it close to Judaism as he understood it. His belief was in the continuity of religious experience. In the year before the "hijra" or the migration to Yathrib (Medina, the city as the Muslims would call it). He prescribed a fast for Muslims on the Jewish day of atonement and commanded Muslims to pray three time a day like the Jews instead of two. Also Muslims could marry Jewish and should observe some of the Jewish dietary laws. Above all, Muslims must pray facing Jerusalem like the Jews and Christians.

(You can see here Muhammad was trying to follow God and do what he thought was right. He wasn't aware of what the Jews knew or how they thought, and he didn't know scripture.) Still today, the Jews are in bondage along with the Muslims. Here I would suggest you read Galatians 4:22–31, verse 29, "Ishmael was born after the flesh and persecuted him that was born after the Spirit as it is now." Muhammad didn't understand how the Jews crucified Christ. Muhammad was just going along with his own understanding. Muhammad was also rejected by the Jews in Medina. The Jews would assemble in the mosque and laugh at the stories and the Muslim religion.

They had knowledge of scripture, and the Muslims didn't; so they would pick holes in the Koran. This was possibly Muhammad's greatest disappointment being rejected by the Jews, calling his whole religious view into question.

Some Jews were friendly with Muhammad, and they helped him with old testament scripture, and how to rebuff the criticisms of other Jews. This was the first time he learned the exact chronology of the prophets. He learned that Abraham had lived before Moses or Jesus. Before this, he may have thought Christians and Jews were of the same religion.

Now he learned there were disagreements between the two. Considering it logical to imagine that the followers of the Torah and the gospel had introduced inauthentic elements into the hanifiyyab, which was the pure religion of Abraham.

Muhammad also found in the old testament their own scripture. They were called faithless people who had turned to idolatry and worshipped a golden calf. Muhammad also got from the Jews the story of Hagar and Ishmael, Abraham's eldest son. How Sarah got jealous and demanded Abraham get rid of her and Ishmael. (Here is where Arabian Jews added some of their own legends. They said Abraham left Hagar in the valley of Mecca where God had later taken care of them, revealing the sacred spring of Zamzam when the child was dying of thirst. Later they say, Abraham visited Ishmael and together they built the first of the one god, "The Kabah.")

With this information, it is a little easier to see the attacks against the Jews and the infidels in the Koran.

In January 624, it became clear that the Jews were hostile thus a *new* religion of Allah declared independence. Muhammad then commanded the Muslims to pray facing Mecca instead of Jerusalem.

By prostrating themselves in the direction of the Kabah, Muslims were declaring that they belonged to no established religion but were surrendering themselves to god alone. They were returning to the primordial religion of Abraham, who they claimed to be the first Muslim to surrender to god and had built the first house.

Prior to this the Jews had temples, Christians had churches, and the Muslims only had shrines in honor of their gods. Now they had a prophet, Muhammad, and Al-ah was the great high god of the pantheon which became their temples or mosques. Their laws coincide with old testament Jewish law though, and whatever they have added or changed over the years. Genesis 12:16 states, "Ishmael would be a wild man in the earth and that his hand would be against every man."

We will now touch on Esau a little. Jacob and Esau were twins, and also the Bible states there were two nations in Rebekah their mother (Genesis 25:23). Nations here comes from the root in the sense of massing—a foreign nation—hence a gentile. Fig: a troop of animals, or a flight of locusts. Heathen nation. Esau was the eldest or the first out. God knew the nature of Esau and hated him.

The custom at the time was to give the birthright or head of the family to the eldest. In this case, Jacob got it. Esau sold his birthright and despised it (Genesis 25:32–34). Later, Jacob received it, and Esau swore revenge against him (Genesis 27:41–42). Reading further, you find out Esau was a rebel. He was angry with Isaac also (Genesis 28:8–9). He went and did something that displeased his father Isaac. He went and married one of Ishmaels daughters. (Now we can see a clearer picture. How Esau told them also how Jacob stole the birthright and treated him unfair according to tradition. Now they both could say how they were betrayed.) Jacob later became Israel after his name change. His sons became known as the children of Israel. They didn't understand God's plan at the time (still don't). It was God's goal. Something he was aiming at to achieve through Jesus Christ. Now the Ishmaelites feel they are entitled to all the blessings and all control.

The Muslims are fighting based upon a religious constitution. Muhammad also became a political leader, not just a religious leader. Islam demands obedience to Al-ah, and the demands are to surrender to their view.

They claim it is a religion of peace but ignore the political aspect of their constitution. The Islamists work together for the purpose of gaining footholds in governments through acceptance. In the process, they are allowed to lie and use deceptive measures to gain trust because it is done in the name of peace for all mankind under their rule. Only the thing in the end, it is getting all to bow to Al-ah and the Islamic law and belief system. They believe they are the chosen and have the pure religion. Their purpose is to grow in numbers and sway governments to honor their views, laws, and cater to them (serve them). In this country, you can somewhat see how this ties in with communism. They have been working with communists in the US coming against free speech, and religious authority they don't acknowledge, working slowly to gain favor. When they build a mosque in an area, they feel it is Al-ah giving them favor, and they are conquering. Notice in this country how airports have built special prayer rooms for them. They are bowing to Al-ah by giving them this privilege, giving them special rights on the job. Many businesses are subsidized if they hire them. This takes Americans jobs. They get half their wages paid for by your taxes. Many leaders have already bowed to Islam. Money they make goes back to their country making nations that hate us rich. While the rights of American citizens are slowly being whittled away to favor those who have different religious beliefs and political views. Their view is against the constitution of the United States of America. They burn our flag and hate this country and Christianity which it was founded upon.

But they do like the favor and especially the money.

Introduction to
Land of the Free

In the previous chapters, we looked at communism and the birth of Islam.

Now we have seen that Islam has their prophet and Imams, the Jews have a high priest, and the Roman church has a pope (Their holy father) or head of the church.

In this chapter, we will look some at the founding and establishing of the United States of America. The reason God allowed the United States to come into existence.

Land of the Free

From Papal Rule

The United States

I will open here with the civil laws that are in place in the US that have been taken out of the Bible and based upon the Ten Commandments. This is not a religion; it is based upon a godly and descent moral code in regards to the way we treat each other.

There were in the old testament no Christians per se as we understand it today. There was a people to whom God gave direction and laws to live by. These being followed kept peace and harmony among the people. At that time, they didn't have the Spirit of God actually living in them as it is today in His church. The laws were given to these people after they had come out of Egypt. They then went into the wilderness, and God began to deal with them on a natural level. They had in Egypt picked up ways of living that were contrary to God and harmony. They needed guidance to get Egypt out of them you could say. In Egypt, things would gook if you honored Pharaoh as god and followed his priest's instructions. Egypt was a very religious nation called the land of the gods. God brought the people out; this is when the Egyptian leaders began to work the people harder. You can read about this in in the book of Exodus. If we go to Genesis 9:4–6, we see a commandment again in relation to the Ten Commandments. This came again after Cain killed Abel his brother.

With this, we can see that actually the laws of the land concerning America have come from scripture going way back. In 1983, *Newsweek* ran an article "How the Bible Formed the Constitution"

(Jesus is King, and we have no King but a constitution with Jesus as King). In order to get God's blessing upon a nation, it was necessary to abide by his principles. Principles of Christianity were joined with civil government (The Ten Commandments became the base for civil law. A government by law not by men. This is why the founding fathers were against a democracy where men ruled and not God. Students could then see the basis for national law.) In 1980, the Ten Commandments were banned in school. This was because a judge claimed a student might read them and obey them. This is not permissible, the court claimed. In 1962 to 1963, reading the Bible and prayer was banned in school. During that time, there was a 460 percent increase in teen pregnancies ages ten to nineteen years of age. When biblical principles were banned, those against marriage rose 1000 percent.

Recalling the communist view (plan) in relation to the family and marriage, you see this playing out. The idea is to create an internal problem subtly to divide a nation. This makes a lot of single mothers, and children who will never know their father. Divorce rates increased, expenses, and more hardship upon the people and within the country.

Going back to England and Europe as well as other countries, the pope and his cardinals ruled not only religion but controlled kings, politics, and government. It was all about submitting to the vatic rule of the pope.

From around 1198 to 1216, there was a problem in England, France, Germany, and throughout Europe when Pope Innocent the third (who claimed to be the vicar of Christ) decreed that "all things are subject to him, including salvation." Pope Innocent is the one who established the term infallibility (which means he can never be wrong or make a mistake). He banned reading the Bible and decreed transubstantiation. This is where they decreed the priest turns a water into Jesus body and wine into his blood (There is one of the places they use scripture out of context to deceive the people). Many believe that because a priest does it!

Luther found out none of the Apostles ever did this (along with other so-called vatic sacraments). It wasn't in the Bible! If people didn't agree with the pope's orders or acknowledge him, they were killed as a heretic. Luther told the pope if he could prove his ideas by the Bible, he would recant his statements against papal rule. The pope couldn't do it. In 1520, Luther was excommunicated because he stood for what the Bible said.

We can see a religious battle has been going on over the years. The people wanted to get away from religious persecution from the political as well as the religious leaders that were in power and governed by the pope. The English authorities were carrying out persecutions against the puritans because they were trying to de-catholicize the church of England. This is what led to the founding of Plymouth in 1620 and the Massachusetts bay colony in 1630.

Let's look for a moment at Columbus. His venture was for a passage of wealth of the Indies. They finally settled for the wealth of the natives. Natives of America whom they called Indians because they thought they were in the Indies. They were looking for wealth being funded by investors. The others were looking for a place where they could worship God and Jesus Christ and have him as the head of the church and not the pope or a man.

William Bradford was a historian who became the leader of Plymouth. When they left on their journey to the Americas, they left with little and trusted God to get them through. In 1620, they came up with the Mayflower compact which some claim to be the first American constitution. This was put together to keep harmony. Forty-one were chosen to sign this agreement or constitution. It opens with, "In the name of God" further to state that their mission is "for the glory of God" and the advancement of the Christian faith. They came from England, and now we can see how we got the New England states.

God's purpose for allowing the United States to come into existence was religious freedom. This freedom was for those who wished to worship God and Jesus Christ according to the Bible and God's principles.

Samuel Adams one of the founding fathers quoted 1 Samuel 2:30, "For them that will honor me, I will honor." This is one of the principles the founders stood on. Principles, God has set down. They believed in the accountability of a nation (A nation under God where people could believe in Christ and live by God's principles). God wanted to raise his church to bring the gospel to the world.

This nation has been blessed because of this. The US has sent more missionaries to the world than any other. The founders put forth effort into applying the constitution and upholding it. Now many of the leaders are taking God out of the schools and trying to regulate what gets preached across the pulpit (When you get down to it, they are trying to regulate religious beliefs, especially Christianity. Then only approving what is legal within society as they see it). They are fighting God who has blessed this country and life itself.

Look at India, if their religious beliefs and their gods are so good, why hasn't their god blessed that that nation?

They turned their backs on God years ago. You don't hear much about Thomas in the Bible after he put his hands in the nail prints of Jesus. Thomas went to India after that with the gospel. A revival took place, and God was moving in that country through the gospel. Thomas was murdered one night while praying. After that, they went back to their old religious ways and beliefs. Since then, India has been on a downhill course. Calcutta is one of the most impoverished cities in the world. Why is this? They fought God and threw out the gospel. This brought the curse back up on the land. They worship everything from bugs to animals and have taken on the theory of reincarnation thinking some animal might be a reincarnated relative.

God says, "He will bless a country that honors Him." The Bible states, "God is a Spirit, and He has a mind." So we are looking at the spiritual side of things here as we go along. Other nations have men's ideas, spawned by the devil and wicked spirits.

After people began coming to America, the Jesuits sent their priests in with some of the immigrants that came here. They brought with them doctrines concerning the pope and his vatic ideas. Many of these people, I believe were sincere in their efforts.

Some of the early preachers of the time never even had a whole Bible. Some had only a few pages, or one that they preached from. Many died on the trail going from town to town with their single page of a Bible.

The devil has always been after the church. He has been trying to stop the word. Why would he be after the church you may ask? Well, the church carries the testimony of Jesus Christ; it is in them. Even looking back at the workings of the pope and vatic rule, the doctrine of the pope's organization fights scripture.

The other teaching of that organization is he is the head of the church, not Jesus. Now it is accepted as a Christian organization. That is not true.

There are Christians in it as members, but the doctrine is not Biblical. Note here, Revelation 13:3, "The beast who's deadly wound was healed." This was papal authority being wounded by Martin Luther who said, "If they by the Bible could prove their doctrine accurate according to scripture, he would recant his statements." They couldn't because the Vatican doctrine is not scriptural. If you note verse two, the dragon gave him his power. In chapter 12:17, the dragon was wroth with the woman (The church that brought forth Sons of God). He made war with her seed, which is Christ.

Tried to take Christ's place and keep the commandments (of love) and have the testimony. The authority or power in 13:2 is judgment and execution of it through religious law. As we know, the Catholic church system destroyed many people and killed them when they wouldn't bow to the pope a supreme religious leader (and political). They have now changed their style to that of being concerned about people on the outside. But there is an inner working going on that is spiritual. We are looking at the spiritual as mentioned earlier. Jesus is Lord and head of the church.

The church needs to stand up and tell the devil, "You can't have America." Speak to the mountain. Many leaders today are listening to the devil. The church or God's people are his target to stop the message of the Lord Jesus Christ to the world.

He already has the Jews; they don't receive Jesus as the Messiah (Some have now though). He is out to stop the testimony of Jesus Christ that is in the true church. God has provided a nation where he can raise his church and be worshipped.

The Spanish armada was the pope's attempt to regain England. The Vatican influenced the king to sail against England. England had a historical victory in 1588; this was the turning point. They claimed for Christian freedom over the power of the papacy in England, Holland, Northern Germany, Denmark, Sweden, and Norway. The founding of Plymouth in 1620 was thirty-two years after the Spanish armada, so this was still fresh to many people. They wanted religious liberty.

The government couldn't do what they are doing today without the approval of the organized church system. Religion lets the beast speak! And they carry out the execution of judgments upon Christians.

They force them to obey laws they dictate. Even in the case where they went after the people who refused to bake a cake for a gay wedding. They over road their right to religious belief based upon God's view of homosexuality found in Leviticus 18:22, "It is an abomination." As mentioned before, it is against nature itself.

The beast system tears you apart and says, "This is our law. We aren't going to see things God's way." Do you see what is going on here? This countries in trouble! What does the organized church do? They sing songs about flying away and don't take a stand with the authority God has given them. The preachers are responsible for the condition of this country and the world. Sadly, most are only preaching what they have been taught and are afraid of losing their congregation. They are afraid of losing the big tithe payers. Well then, how would they make a living right? They do it for a career. We are to give to support the gospel (Good news the kingdom is come and Christ is here in his people). Many are giving to Judas. He sold out Christ. See John 12:6 and 13:29. Judas had the bag. Judas was the accountant and handled the finances. Remember, Judas sold out for thirty pieces of silver. The theologians who have gone beyond their measure have sold the church to the world for money and a position in society (they water the message down for a price). We can get a deeper meaning of 1 Timothy 6:10 now, "The love of money is the root of all evil." Which they have coveted after and they have errored from the faith. Concerned about a big church and not the message and the people. Because of this, government has moved in and brought in other doctrines and the like and have undermined this country and constitution.

Now we have Muslims in the government with no allegiance to this country and feel their god is giving them the victory. The pledge of allegiance has now been banned in public places signed in by Obama. Is this God? What country is as patient with people in the line of rights?

> There is a battle going on over
> Whose god or gods or ideas
> Get to control the world
> As for me and my house
> We will serve the *Lord!*

Introduction to
God's Promises to Believers

͜෨ळ෨ळ͡

Where do we go from here? What do we do?
What can we do when it appears hopeless?
I will do my best to answer these questions.
  There is hope. There is victory
  Through the Promises of God.

God's Promises to Believers

We have seen from the previous chapters how Islam, the Vatican, and other belief systems through them are trying to reach God or please God. These we know are based upon tradition and or the teachings of men.

Note in Matthew 23:1–5, verse three, "The leaders, religious lawmakers (Moses seat) tell you what to observe." [Which in the Greek means: A watch, to guard (from loss or injury by keeping an eye on) implies to a prophecy.] Fig: meaning to fulfill a command, and to keep unmarried: hold fast-keepserve-watch. To detain in custody. Fig: maintain.

Jesus is saying they command you to adhere to church law and the rules to please God. The leaders of mainstream religion speak and teach what they have been taught (to teach they offer a form of worship and rituals like genuflecting to the altar, wearing a hat to church for women and how to dress, things like that). Jeremiah 23:16–17 states, "They speak a vision of their own heart." What they see and think is right. See also Jeremiah 14:11–14, verse fourteen, They prophecy lies. They prophecy peace to people who don't even care about serving God. The things you are hearing is about uniting all people and religions to obtain world peace.

In that you see all the traditions of any religion, belief, or practice as something God accepts. In the wake of this are scriptures they have chosen to line up with their belief system. It is what they agree to for their own justification.

The penalty for disagreeing is: They kick you out and make you feel you are going to hell if you are not a follower with them. (1 Peter 4:1–4, They think it strange that you do not run with them to the same excess of riot, speaking evil of you.) Riot meaning "unsaved-ness" ie. [by imp.] profligacy or excess.

Profligacy meaning wildly extravagant, given to dissipation and licentiousness—prodigal. Dissipation is the act of dissipating meaning to separate into parts and scatter or vanish. They think you have left following God if you don't adhere to their traditions. Maybe you got some faith and are looking for greener pastures. (Christ says in Revelation, I will remove your candle stick. I will take my people out from you.)

The Catholic church had what was called mortal sin and venial sin. Mortal sin was against the church which was greater than a venial sin (It was a sin against their law and doctrine laid down by the pope and his taskmasters). They claimed it couldn't be forgiven.

A venial sin was against God and could be forgiven (Of course by one of the priests ordained by the officials of their church. This official would give you penance to do and then you'd be forgiven the next time right). So they are teaching; it is a priest who has the power to forgive sins, instead of you just going to God and Christ on your own. He is the one who died for you. This religious stuff is hog wash!

It is a doctrine of men from the pits of hell, denying the works of Christ. His blood cleanses us from all sin. Not penance a priest gives you! See 1 John 2:1 where it states, "We have an advocate before the Father." In 1 John 1:9, it says, "You go directly to God and He will cleanse you of sin." I hope you can see this religious deception that is in this system. It appeases the conscience, and that is about all it does along with satisfying the emotions for a while. People always say they were baptized into… And that is what rules, what they are baptized into. A denomination of religion, all of the traditions, rules and adherence to them does keep some form of order, or you could say disorderly order. It strips you of your power and really coming to know the love of God through Christ. Isaiah 28:7 states, "They err in vision and stumble in judgment." We have seen much of this err in judgment, especially in the approval of homosexuality as well as accepting Muhammad's belief system relating to a religion of peace.

Relation to peace is referring to submission to old testament law, and others they have made up and thrown in. 1 Galatians 4:22–25, it states, "The Jews are also in bondage with the Ishmaelites." (Hagar or Agar) They are both waiting for the redeemer or the twelfth Imam. (I hope you will check this out in your Bible) Verse twenty-six, Jerusalem which is above is free. Now we are seeing this is spiritual. The word *free* in the Greek meaning, "unrestrained (to go at pleasure)" i.e. as a citizen not a slave. Here see Hebrews 4:14–16, "Come boldly unto the throne of grace." Free also means "exempt from obligation or liability." Jesus said, "The true worshippers must worship God in spirit…" (John 4:24).

This doesn't mean there is a license to sin, or we can do whatever we want. It means we can walk and live in a way that pleases God. We can receive our inheritance in Christ (our foundation as an heir with Him). Claim God's promises, thank him for them, and do the works of Christ.

Concerning what is going on in the world today, we will find much uncertainty. Look at the Mideast, wars and threats by terrorism. God is cleaning house.

Isaiah 30:31–32 states, "For through the voice of the LORD shall the Assyrian be beaten down, which smote with a rod. And in every place where the grounded staff shall pass, which the LORD shall lay upon him, it shall be with tabrets and harps. And in battles of shaking will He fight with it."

We also see in Luke 6:47–49, concerning the wise man who built his house upon a rock. How it was shaken and didn't fall because it was founded upon a rock (The revelation of Christ being the rock or foundation). Not Peter like the church of Rome teaches. God builds his house upon Christ his Son, not a man. Peter was actually never in Rome. We through Christ stand on his word. We believe he can't lie. Isn't that great! Check out Hebrews 6:17–19, "We are heirs of the promise."

What then are the promises? Let's look at the ninety-first Psalm for some (there are many).

> No evil shall befall thee
> Neither any plague come nigh thy dwelling
> Gives his angels charge over us
> With long life I will satisfy him and show him
> my salvation
> Verse fourteen, because he has known my name.
> What then is the name?

Name refers to the word of God. See Revelation 19:13, "His name is called the word of God." We as believers know and believe the word of God. We receive through believing and receiving through Christ and his works. He came to destroy the works of the devil. We are now under grace not under the law.

We need to stand up and be God's voice in the earth, speak to the mountain. The church has been taught they are going to fly away. That is confusion and mistranslation totally out of context. They say you shall have peace and just float away without even having any faith or doing anything for the kingdom.

Jesus said in John 16:33, "In this world you shall have tribulation." In Acts 14:22, "Through much tribulation you will enter into the kingdom of God." Tribulation is outside pressure to turn from your faith and what God has shown you. Tribulation can be getting kicked out of your church, alienated from your family, and pressure to quit moving with God. If you turn back, it is like a dog returning to his own vomit according to 2 Peter 2:22.

Revelation 7:14–17 relates to those who came out of great tribulation, and God wipes away all their tears. Many ask how do I come out? Quit fighting with these people first.

Quit believing religious lies and philosophies. Believe God and what he says about you. You come out by entering in, enter into a new spirit of Christ, and relax. Stand on his promises and what Christ has done for you now. In 1 Peter 2:24, it says, "With his stripes you are healed." In Timothy, it states, "You have a sound mind." We come to a place of rest in him. He in us; we in him, and our lives are hid with Christ in God according to Colossians 3:3.

Jesus said in Luke 10:19, "Nothing by any means shall hurt you."

"This is the victory that overcometh the world, even our Faith" (1 John 5:4).

About the Author

S ince returning from Vietnam where he was in Army Aviation, Pat Skinner continued with art, logo design, autobody, and motorcycle customizing. In the mid-90s, the author got involved with natural medicine and became the president of the International Association of Physicians for Minnesota in 1996.

Since 1984, Pat began radio messages and Bible studies. He has been speaking in Minnesota and Texas. Presently, the author is sharing the message in seminars, treatment centers, and churches with alcoholics and drug addicts.

CPSIA information can be obtained
at www.ICGtesting.com
Printed in the USA
LVHW050027240919
631983LV00004B/746/P